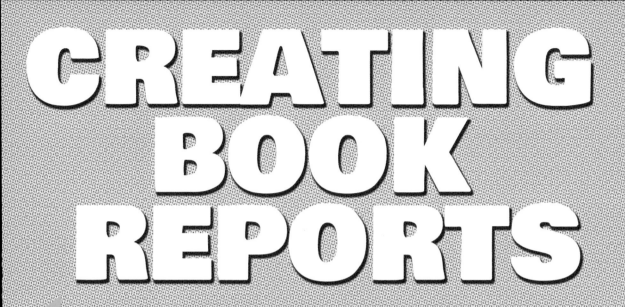

CREATING BOOK REPORTS

WITH COOL NEW DIGITAL TOOLS

GINA HAGLER

rosen publishing's
rosen central®

NEW YORK

Published in 2014 by The Rosen Publishing Group, Inc.
29 East 21st Street, New York, NY 10010

Library of Congress Cataloging-in-Publication Data

Hagler, Gina.
Creating book reports with cool new digital tools/by Gina Hagler.
p. cm. — (Way beyond PowerPoint: making 21st century presentations)
Includes bibliographical references and index.
ISBN 978-1-4777-1834-6 (library binding) — ISBN 978-1-4777-1845-2 (pbk.) — ISBN 978-1-4777-1846-9 (6-pack)
1. Report writing — Juvenile literature. 2. Book reviewing — Juvenile literature. 3. Presentation graphics software — Juvenile literature. I. Hagler, Gina. II. Title.
LB1047.3 H34 2014
372.13028–dc23

Manufactured in the United States of America

CPSIA Compliance Information: Batch #W14YA: For further information, contact Rosen Publishing, New York, New York, at 1-800-237-9932.

CONTENTS

INTRODUCTION

Book reports have been part of school life for decades. They've had much the same format for decades, too. You start with information such as the name of the book, the name of the author, and the genre. Throw in some details about the main character. Give a synopsis, along with whether or not you'd recommend this book and why. You know the drill.

In the nineteenth century, students committed poems to memory and recited them before the class with nothing but the words in their heads. Skip ahead a hundred years or so and a student presenting a report might clutch a piece of paper with notes. Index cards and flip charts came next.

Fast-forward to the twenty-first century. We may not have jetpacks or flying cars, but there are some new ways to tell the class about the book you've read. Depending on the software you use, you can make a movie, create a podcast, or host a book talk. You can also create an animation, a series of diagrams, a polished slideshow, or a soundtrack inspired by the book. All you need is a computer, possibly a video camera and microphone, and some time to try out the features of the software before you begin. After that, it's simply a matter of envisioning your book report as a presentation, adding some extra information—such as an interactive timeline—to give it some punch, and you're ready to begin.

With the right software, equipment, and a bit of planning, it's not hard to replace index cards with a remote control in your hand. This book will look at what it takes to create a rich presentation, rather than a simple book report. It will focus on the software that is available, the equipment that you will need, and the features that will make a difference to you. Ready to talk about how to plan your presentation and put that plan into action? Let's go!

Students review the work they've done on their digital
book report.

THE BOOK REPORT

The book report: you probably know it well. It's a time-tested method for capturing all relevant information so that your teacher can see what you've garnered from your reading. It's also a way to inform the rest of the class about the book you've just read, maybe even enticing a few classmates to read it themselves. You cover the basics, give a synopsis, and add your personal opinion. When it's time to tell your classmates about your book and present your book report, it's likely you will stand at the front of the room and read from a paper in your hand.

But what if you could do more? What if you could think bigger than a poster, diorama, or pile of index cards? What if you could create a book report that has the class waiting breathlessly to see what happens next? What if you could go digital and bring the book report into this century? What if you could bring your book report to life? You can. This book will show you how. But before we explore book reports in the digital age, we need to cover the purpose and the elements of a book report.

PURPOSE OF A BOOK REPORT

A book report is designed to serve several purposes. The obvious purpose is to ensure you fulfill your commitment to read the book you've been assigned or have chosen to read. After all, it's hard to give a report and answer questions about a book you haven't read. Another purpose is to bring information about your book to the other students in your class. It's possible that one of them will hear your report and become interested in reading the book, too.

A well-done book presentation will surely capture the attention of your classmates.

Book reports are also designed to help students learn about the author or genre. By closely examining books by the same author or in the same genre, you can learn about what it takes to be a successful writer. For example, you'll see if the author of your current book writes mainly in one genre. If so, are there other books in the series that you would like to read? Are there recurring characters? Does the story of the characters take place over one book or several? You'll discover all of these are things while doing the work for your book report.

7

8

The setting is an important part of a book. In a digital book report, you can include images that bring the setting to life, as this farm image does for a book like *Charlotte's Web*.

Enticing your classmates to read the book you've just finished is another point of the report. This is trickier than it sounds. You could write a report that makes the book sound like the best book ever. However, if you overdo it, you won't sound authentic, and it is unlikely anyone will touch that book. You need to be honest and fair. You have to pick the aspects of the book that made you happy you read it. Then write about them in a way that makes your classmates want to have the same experience. At the same time, you have to be careful not to give so much away that other people don't see a reason to pick it up for themselves. None of that is easy with paper, shoeboxes, and poster board—the tools typically at hand for a conventional book report.

Displaying your knowledge is yet another purpose of the book report. It isn't enough that you've read the book. It isn't even enough that you can answer the basic questions included in a book report. Have you given careful thought to the author's writing style or the genre? What have you taken away from the characters or the plot? What's going to stay with you after you've read the book? These are the things that your teacher and classmates are waiting to hear. These details will help them determine if you got anything out of the book and if the book might be something they'd like to read, too.

ELEMENTS OF A BOOK REPORT

Book reports are all very similar. There are certain pieces of information that are typically included. As a rule, these are the elements of a book report:

I. Basic Information
- **Title.** Include the entire title and the subtitle (the part of the title after the colon), if any.
- **Author.** List the first name and last name of all authors.
- **Illustrator.** If the book is illustrated, include the illustrator's first name and last name.
- **Publisher.** You'll find the publisher's name on the title page in the front of the book.
- **Publication date.** This is found on the copyright page in the front of the book.
- **Number of pages.** Use the page numbers, or look at the contents page in the front of the book.
- **Genre.** Genres, such as mystery, adventure, or science fiction, categorize the book and help readers know what to expect. If you're not sure of your book's genre, discuss it with your librarian or teacher.

II. Fundamental Information
- **Main characters' names.** These should be their full names.
- **Main character description.** Include details that help us understand and remember each main character.
- **Description of other important characters.** Don't forget the sidekick!
- **Setting (location).** This is where the story takes place. Desert or rainforest, city or farm, it's important to tell your classmates the setting so that they can better picture the action.
- **Setting (time).** Is the book set in the future, the past, or the present? What are the exact years or the general time period? Your

classmates need to know this so that they can understand the context of the events.

- **Setting (other).** Include anything else that's important in helping your classmates understand the setting of the story. For example, the main character may live within a particular culture or community.
- **Series information.** If your book is part of a series, mention that in your report.
- **Prior events.** If things happened in earlier titles that readers must know in order to understand and enjoy the book, briefly include that information.

III. Synopsis

- **Plot summary.** Give a basic summary of what happens, especially the central problem the main character faces. At the same time, don't give it all away. Movie critics leave people hanging, and so should you.
- **Theme or main idea.** If the story had a moral, life lesson, or other main point, explain it.
- **Teaser.** Include something that will make your classmates want to read the book for themselves.

IV. Personal Opinion or Review

- **Recommendation.** Do you think the book is worth reading? If so, tell your classmates.
- **Reasons.** Explain why the book is worth reading (or in some cases, why it isn't). Talk about its strengths and weaknesses. Describe the kinds of readers that would probably enjoy it most.
- **Other books.** If you've read other books like this one that you could recommend, mention them. How do those other books compare to this one?

While these are typical elements that students must cover in a report, it's possible your teacher may require other pieces of information as well. Be sure to double-check before you begin.

ORGANIZING YOUR INFORMATION DIGITALLY

Digital tools give you the opportunity to create a whole new type of book report. Your report can include music, videos, photos, artwork—pretty much anything you can think of that relates to the book. The first step in creating a book report is gathering and organizing your information. Why not organize your information digitally?

Evernote is one of a number of software applications that save and organize your notes.

Evernote is software that captures your ideas, notes, images, Web pages, and more. You can give this input tags for easy searching. You can create a "notebook," or file, for a project and put all related inputs into that notebook. Since the information is stored in the cloud (on the Internet), you can access the information in your account from a variety of devices, not just your home computer. Evernote offers apps for the iPhone, iPad, and Droid. The first step is to create an account. (But never create an online account without your parents' permission!) Some services are free, while those considered "premium" cost money. You can find out more information at the Mac App Store or at the Evernote Web site (https://evernote.com).

OneNote is very similar to Evernote. It is not free, but if you have Office for Windows, it may be available to you. You can store your information in the cloud by means of a SkyCloud account. This allows you to access your account from a Windows computer, Windows phone, iPhone, iPad, or Droid. The first step is to open an account. You can get more information at the Microsoft OneNote Web site (http://office.microsoft.com/en-us/onenote).

Using a digital information storage system such as Evernote or OneNote allows you to pull information from various sources directly into a digital notebook or project file. Later, when it's time to go back and review information, you can easily search for particular words or phrases. If you want to revisit a site, you can click on the link. When it's time to review your images, they will be right there in your project file.

WHAT IF YOU DON'T LIKE THE BOOK?

Relax. The truth is, not all books are good. Even books that are well regarded are not right for every reader. If you didn't like the book that you read, that's OK. If you can change books, try to switch to another one. If you've left yourself no time for that, prepare your book report with all the information required. When it comes time to give a recommendation, it's fine to say that you don't recommend the book. The important part is to give your reasons. Give specific examples of the things that didn't work for you. For example, you may dislike a book because of the characters or message. Perhaps the main character had negative traits and was so unlikable that you found it difficult to care what happened to him. Perhaps the book's theme was overly optimistic or pessimistic.

Be sure to include anything that did work for you, too. If you think the book was well written but the genre wasn't for you, say so. If you think the genre and plot were good but the writing was weak, say that. It might just be the case that someone else in the class will like the book for the very reasons that you didn't. For that reason alone, it's important to be fair and specific.

THE BOOK REPORT AS A PRESENTATION

You may think of presenting a book report as a chore. It is something you have to do and not something you expect to enjoy. With that outlook, preparing and presenting your book report is likely to feel more like a punishment than an opportunity to flex your creative muscles.

How about changing your view of book reports? A book report is a chance to prepare and deliver a presentation that you're proud of. It's

Viewing your book report as a multimedia presentation opens a world of new possibilities.

a chance to communicate not only the standard information but a bit more in a way that gets your classmates to sit up and pay attention. It's also a great opportunity to take advantage of all the technology available to you.

WHAT IS A PRESENTATION?

A presentation is one way of delivering information to an audience. It is an organized approach to sharing your information. It is often scripted, meaning that you've worked out in advance what you're going to say. It often makes use of visual aids, such as a slideshow, or objects from the setting described in the book. There is often a time limit on the length of a presentation. The flow of information in a presentation is easy to follow because the person presenting the information has planned it all out.

There are many types of presentations. The slideshow is one popular type. With a slideshow, the person making the presentation uses PowerPoint or another software application to prepare slides. These contain basic information that the presenter wants to deliver to the

Slideshows are an excellent way to share information about your reading while inviting audience participation.

audience. The slides may include images from the book or photos of places that have to do with the book. If there is no explanatory text included on the slide, the presenter will explain each slide as it appears on the screen.

The question-and-answer session (often called a Q&A) can be an important part of a presentation. In a Q&A, the person presenting the information answers questions posed by an interviewer or the people in the room. The challenge in a question-and-answer session is to stay on track. Typically, the person making the presentation will deliver all of the basic information about the author and book and then take questions at the end.

A book talk is another excellent way to make a presentation about a book. In a book talk, the presenter first delivers the basic information about the book. Then he or she tells the audience more about the author, setting or time period, or other related books. This additional information brings more meaning to the book report.

WHAT DO BOOK REPORT PRESENTATIONS INCLUDE?

Presentations include basic information about the book, along with details that give the report more depth. For example, the presenter might discuss other books by the author if they are related to the book in some meaningful way. Discussion of recurring characters or themes may be part of the presentation. Bits of the music of the time can be included. So can images of the setting of the book. The presenter may also describe events that were taking place at the time in which the story is set.

When selecting additional pieces of information to include, the key is to choose details that add meaning to the presentation. Maybe they will give the audience a better sense of what the book is about or help them understand why reading the book is worthwhile. Maybe they will help the audience understand the era in which the action takes place or why the characters make the choices they do. It's up to you.

In addition to music, book report presentations can include film clips, newspaper headlines, and a timeline of the book and/or the life of the author.

Photos, graphs, and charts can be used to convey information in a digital book report.

Charts can be included if they are helpful in getting your information across. The charts can even have moving parts if the program you use to create the presentation has that capability. Similarly, you can design animations and timelines to reveal greater detail when you click on them. You have a wide array of options available to you that can add interest and value to your presentation.

19

MAKE A TRAILER FOR YOUR BOOK REPORT

You've seen trailers for movies. They are designed to reveal just enough about the movie to get you interested, yet not so much that you decide you no longer need to go to the theater to see it. The same is true of a book trailer.

Videos created in iMovie can be viewed on a number of devices.

Your book trailer won't be made up of scenes from a movie, but it can include video you create. You can do this by using an application such as iMovie. This application allows you to use individual photos or video to present compelling information about your book.

Whether you use photographs or a video, you can include a voiceover in which a narrator speaks about what is being shown. You can also include music in the background. The specific music is up to you. You can use it to fade in, fade out, or be part of the entire presentation. You can even choose to feature the music for one or more parts of the trailer.

Remember, the goal of the trailer is to use audio and visual techniques to hook viewers on the book.

WHY MAKE THIS EXTRA EFFORT?

Preparing a full presentation using multimedia tools, rather than going the traditional oral report route, takes time. So why bother?

1. **You can present more information.** Including visual information allows your audience to see what you're talking about, making it easier to explain the details. You can use an image and then talk about the important parts of that image.

2. **You can give your audience a fuller understanding of the time and place of the book.** Rather than just telling your audience that your book takes place during the Jazz Age, you can include bits of music, pictures of the clothing, and headlines from the newspapers of the time. These artifacts will make the time period real to your audience.

3. **Your report will be more interesting.** Using digital tools allows you to add music, interactive features, and video clips to your report. If

you use these wisely, they'll make your presentation more engaging to your audience.

4. **You can use your creativity.** This is your chance to come up with a great idea and bring it to life. Your book report can be whatever you can envision and create.

PLANNING IS ESSENTIAL

You can dive right in and begin your report without any forethought. Or you can give it a bit of thought beforehand, find the right applications for what you want to achieve, get your equipment together, and set out to create your vision.

By planning the presentation up front, there's a much better chance you'll have what you need and be ready by the deadline. You can also ensure that you include everything the assignment requires, along with additional content to bring your presentation to life. You'll be able to make sure all of your efforts fit together, resulting in an amazing book presentation.

Some presenters create a kind of storyboard. With this approach, they use images or words to plan out a beginning, middle, and end to their presentation. This way, the overall game plan is in place. Then they fill in the details of what will occur between those key points. They decide up front that they'd like to include songs or fashions from the time, for example. What is left is finding just the right songs or images to create the strongest possible digital book report.

SOFTWARE APPLICATIONS THAT DO THE WORK

Making your book report into a digital presentation that others can view on a screen at the front of the room, or even on their own computers, sounds like a terrific idea. You're looking forward to giving it a try. In fact, you've got a plan in mind and know what sort of presentation you'd like to create. Now you just need to decide on a software application (program) that can do the job.

The way to know if a software application will do what you need it to do is to check out the features of the program. To make this easier, we'll discuss the types of applications available, along with the equipment you'll need, so that you can confidently decide on the right application for your digital book report.

THE RIGHT PROGRAM MAKES A DIFFERENCE

There are many different types of software applications. Some are ideal for creating a slideshow, while others are especially good for creating animations. Some excel at diagrams, while others make making movies easy. Still others help you design flyers and diagrams that go far beyond what you could do by hand or within a word processing program.

Some software programs run directly on your computer, and others are Web-based, or used online. With desktop software, look on the box or in the description of the software on the company's Web site to see if it will run on your computer. Once you're certain it can run on your machine—or that you can use it online—you need to determine if the

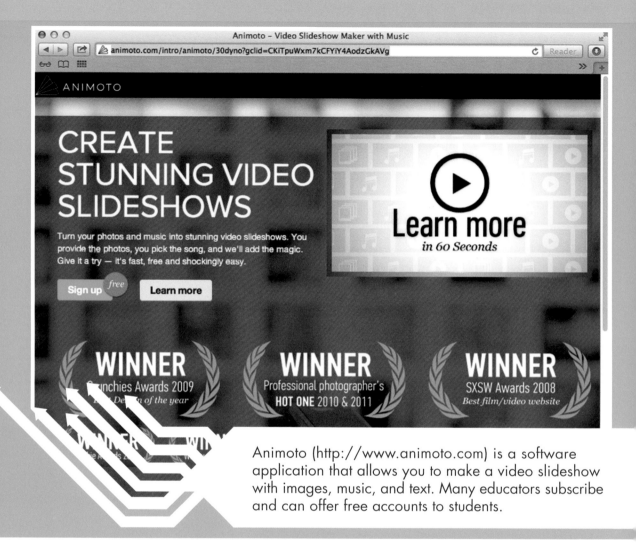

Animoto (http://www.animoto.com) is a software application that allows you to make a video slideshow with images, music, and text. Many educators subscribe and can offer free accounts to students.

program can do the type of work that you want. The program features are usually listed in the description of the software application, either on the box or on the Web site for that software. Some features that you may be looking for are the ability to make movies from video or images, create animations, create slideshows with music, and design charts or diagrams. You may also want to know if an application is suited to creating stories.

Check to see if there is a cost for the software or the finished product. Some software must be purchased. Some products offer a free project as a trial offer. It's up to you to be sure you understand the terms and whether or not the software you are using is truly free.

It's also a great idea to explore the offerings of your school or public library. Many of today's libraries lend hardware and software tools to students and others in the community. Some even have special centers for the creation of multimedia projects. Librarians can direct you toward the best tools for your project.

POSSIBLE PROGRAMS FOR YOUR DIGITAL BOOK REPORT

The exact program you decide to work with will depend on the type of digital book report you have in mind. If you're planning to make a movie, you will need a movie-making program. For animation or slideshows, you will need programs that can help you create those kinds of presentations. Other types of digital book reports will require other programs.

Be sure to consider the kind of equipment you'll be using. To make a video, for example, you will need some sort of video recorder. It will be important to select a software program that works with that device.

The following are some types of programs that you may find useful for your digital book report:

MOVIE MAKING

Apple's iMovie is a software application for the Mac. The software is installed and runs on a computer, rather than on the Web. It includes a number of predesigned templates, or styles, for your movie. It also offers music that you can use in the background. You can use music of your own, too. You can also include audio in which you do the talking.

Animoto, Stupeflix, and WeVideo are all Web-based, so you create your movie while online. You can combine photos and video clips that go with your report, perhaps a reenactment of an exciting scene in the book. You have control over many things as you create your movie. You select the style for your movie, the music, and the text that will appear. It's also easy to share a movie with others via the Web.

ANIMATION

Voki is an online program that allows you to create an avatar—a graphic image—to present your book report. The application walks you through the process of creating a customized avatar. Select a background, create your voice, and you're ready to create an animated version of your book report.

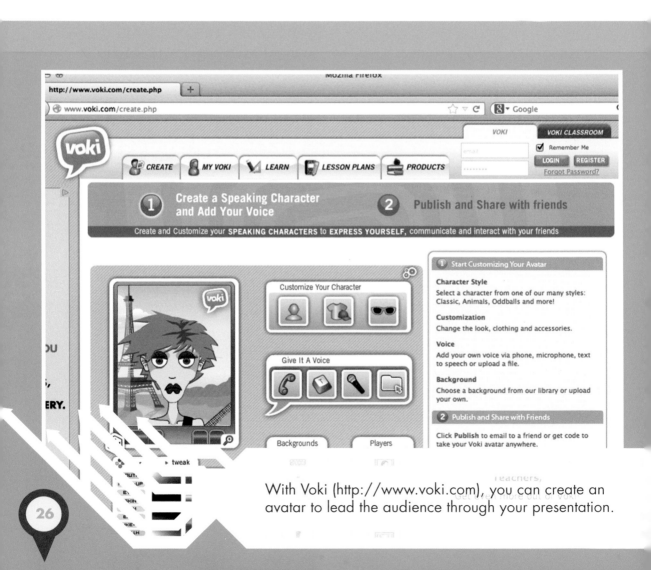

With Voki (http://www.voki.com), you can create an avatar to lead the audience through your presentation.

You can also create an animated book report with GoAnimate. Again, you create characters, a background, and voices for your characters and record what they have to say. You can also use your own voice to create a voiceover. Your finished product can easily be shared over the Web.

SLIDESHOWS

Microsoft PowerPoint, Google Presentation, Apple's Keynote, and Prezi are all slideshow applications. PowerPoint and Keynote reside on your computer, while Google Presentation and Prezi are Web-based. But they all allow you to create slides to tell your story. You can embed videos and images in your presentation, along with the text slides you use to inform your audience about your book. Juxio and SlideSnack can also be used to create slideshows. Presentations created with these applications are intended for distribution over the Web.

FLYERS AND DIAGRAMS

Smore is an excellent Web-based program for creating custom flyers. There are a number of graphics and fonts available. You can include photos and graphics in your flyer, too. The result is a product that adds more interest to your book report. When done, you can print out your flyer or share it online.

Sometimes you need a diagram to tell your story. It may help explain the plot or the way that historical events impacted the time period of your story. With Cacoo, a Web-based diagramming program, you can create intricate diagrams easily. The finished product can be used in a presentation or shared on the Web.

STORIES

With Little Bird Tales, you can create an online book in a Web-based program. You upload your own artwork, images, text, and voice to tell a story. In this case, the story will be your book report. Clicking "play" on the finished product begins the presentation.

SOFTWARE APPLICATION FEATURES

The trick to picking the right software for your task is to match the features of the software with your needs. One way to do that is to make a table listing the features that are important to you and filling in the blanks. In the table below, you can see that someone who wants to make a movie in a Web-based program with easy sharing capabilities would not use iMovie because it doesn't have those features.

Software	Function	Web-Based	Easy Share	Equipment
iMovie	Movie	No	No	Video/Audio
Animoto	Movie	Yes	Yes	Video/Camera
Stupeflix	Movie	Yes	Yes	Video/Camera
WeVideo	Movie	Yes	Yes	Video/Camera
Voki	Animation	Yes	Yes	Audio
GoAnimate	Animation	Yes	Yes	Audio
PowerPoint	Slideshow	No	No	None
Google Presentation	Slideshow	Yes	Yes	None
Keynote	Slideshow	No	No	None
Prezi	Slideshow	Yes	Yes	None
Juxio	Slideshow	Yes	Yes	None
SlideSnack	Slideshow	Yes	Yes	None
Smore	Flyer	Yes	Yes	None
Cacoo	Diagram	Yes	Yes	None
Little Bird Tales	Story	Yes	Yes	Scanner/Audio
Storybird	Story	Yes	Yes	Scanner/Audio

Storybird is another online product for creating digital stories. The star in the story is your artwork or other images, so Storybird is excellent if you have a strong visual storyline in mind for your book report.

Both of these applications create presentations that can be shared on the Web. If you want to upload original artwork that was not created digitally, you'll also need a scanner.

EQUIPMENT

The equipment—specifically, computer accessories—that you will need to prepare your book report depends on the type of presentation you are planning. Here are some types of equipment that you might need:

- **Video.** If you want to make a video or include video clips in your presentation, you will need a video camera of some kind. This can range from the camera in your smartphone to a digital camera with video capabilities to a FlipCam or video camera. Any of these will work well for your needs.

- **Audio.** If your plans call for the sound of your voice in the book report presentation, you will need a device that captures audio as you create a video (all the video options mentioned so far do) or a separate means of capturing audio. That can be the microphone built into your computer or one that you plug into it.

- **Scanner.** Scanners range from flatbed to handheld types. Many all-in-one printers have scanning capability. As long as your scanner can capture and save images so that you can get them onto your computer, you are all set.

- **Other equipment.** If you're making a video on a windy day, you may want to shield the camera's microphone so that the sound of the wind is not louder than the voices in the video. You may also want

The equipment you need will depend upon the type of presentation you plan to make. Check with your school or local library to see if you can borrow the needed equipment.

some additional lighting sources if you are making a video inside and the lighting is not bright enough for good images.

Have you decided to go with an animation, slideshow, flyer, diagram, or storytelling presentation without your personal voice? You may not need any special equipment aside from a computer, but you will need an Internet connection and the ability to upload your images to the Web.

Take some time to try out the equipment before you start working on your project. There may be special effects that you can use but hadn't thought about. Or the site you chose for filming or recording may not be ideal. For example, you may notice that there is a lot of background noise in your test recordings. By trying out your equipment and techniques beforehand, you'll be able to get it right when it counts the most.

STRUT YOUR STUFF

The day of the presentation is your chance to share your digital book report with an audience. It's likely the presentation will take place in your classroom with your classmates as the audience. In past presentations, you may have rushed through so that you could go back to your seat as soon as possible. Suppose you imagine things a bit differently this time. Imagine this as the first of many outstanding presentations you will make. With the right attitude and preparation, your presentation may be effective enough to get your classmates to read the book or other books by the same author. With that in mind, let's take a look at what you'll need to truly strut your stuff.

PRESENTATION SKILLS

You can have the greatest presentation in the history of digital book reports. Your book report can have music, videos, animations, and slides with a unique template. However, none of that will matter if you have poor presentation skills. Nobody enjoys a presentation by someone who is hesitant and clearly wishes he or she could run from the room. When you give a presentation, be sure to:

- **Make eye contact.** Look at your audience and speak directly to them.
- **Speak in a loud voice.** You don't need to yell, but you do need to speak loudly enough so that even the people in the back of the room can hear you.

Relax when giving your presentation. Make eye contact, and enjoy your time in the spotlight.

- **Speak clearly.** This is not the time to mumble or speak into your chin.
- **Speak at a normal rate.** Don't try to get through all of your comments in record time. Practice with a timer so that you know your presentation fills the required time.
- **Leave time for questions.** If your audience has a few questions at the end of your presentation, that's a good thing. It means you've caught their attention and made them wonder about some things you didn't address. If there are no questions, use that time to thank the group for being such a good audience.

- **Don't be afraid to say you don't know the answer.** No one knows everything about a topic. You may know a great deal, yet someone may still ask you something you haven't considered or come across in your research. Don't panic. Acknowledge that it's a good question. If you can make a good guess based on your research, say it's a guess and share your thoughts. If not, say that you'll look into it.

Finally, remember to breathe. This may be easier said than done, but try to relax and enjoy telling your audience all that you have discovered about your book and author.

BE PREPARED

It's not easy to relax if you're unsure that your equipment is in place or is functioning correctly. Ask ahead. See if there will be a computer in the room that you can use and if that computer has the software you'll need. Be sure to have the proper media to save your file and transfer it to that computer. If you used a Web-based software application, be sure that you have the necessary passwords to access your online account.

Will you project your presentation onto a screen or whiteboard? Maybe you have access to an interactive whiteboard, such as a Promethean board or SMART board. Find out beforehand and see if you can practice a bit with the equipment if you're unsure how it works. Also ask if it's your job to be sure that everything you need is there, or if the teacher will have all the equipment in the room on the report presentation days.

Know exactly how much time you will have for your presentation. Check the assignment sheet or rubric, or ask the teacher. It is your job to complete your digital book report in the allotted time. It's not good to finish too early—or too late. Your presentation should come in right on time.

Practice—often. Practice on your own. Practice in front of your family. Time yourself so that you know about how far you should be in your report at intervals throughout the presentation. To make sure you are speaking loudly enough, ask a family member to sit as far away as the back of the classroom.

Practice your presentation, including using the multi-media equipment. When it's your turn, you'll feel more comfortable and confident.

35

Then say what you have to say and see if that family member can hear you. You may have to project your voice more than you think.

STRONG BEGINNINGS AND ENDINGS

Sure, you could get up in front of the class, switch on the projector, and launch right into your presentation. However, it's good to give a brief introduction first, something that sets the stage for your presentation. It can be as simple as giving the title and author of the book that you are reporting on and saying that you've created a book talk in iMovie and you hope they enjoy it. Whatever your remarks, tie them in to your presentation. The introduction will give you a moment to collect yourself before you begin. It will also give your audience a chance to direct their attention to what you have to share.

There are bound to be people in the group with questions. In your introduction, you can mention whether or not you'll take questions at the end. You can ask the audience to hold any questions until this time. This is a good idea so that you don't get sidetracked during your presentation. Remember that questions are usually not meant to challenge you. They are things that are puzzling your audience. Give a polite answer. If you don't know the answer, say so. There's nothing wrong with that—unless it's the title of the book or the name of the author!

Plan a few concluding words to wrap up your presentation after the question period, and you'll end on a strong note.

HANDOUTS AND SWAG

One way to grab the attention of an audience is to give handouts or other items. However, make sure that whatever you give out does not distract your audience. You want people's attention to be on you. You also need to be sure that whatever you give the audience relates directly to your digital book report.

A handout created in Smore may be just the thing. You can be certain to include key information and images that tie in to what you have to say. In fact, this handout could be part of your introduction. Diagrams created with Cacoo could also become handouts. Finally, printouts with the slides of a slideshow

WHAT MAKES A GOOD HANDOUT?

Good handouts provide useful information to your audience. They:
- Are visually appealing.
- Are not cluttered with information.
- Get right to the point.
- Directly tie in to your presentation.
- Give additional information about the book or author.
- Provide background information about your book's setting or time period.
- Reinforce what you've said about your genre or book.

can be useful as well. They give the audience a chance to make notes on the slides as they hear what you have to say.

What else can you give out? You might distribute Halloween candy if the book is about Halloween or fortune cookies if the book is set in Chinatown. Use your imagination. Just keep it simple and tied in to your presentation. Be sure to ask your teacher for permission beforehand.

SHARING YOUR PRESENTATION

Digital book reports make a great presentation for your class. They are also great for uploading to Web sites such as YouTube and Vimeo. Doing this allows other people—including people you've never met—to see your work. They can leave comments and questions, too. This gives you a chance to gain a larger audience for what you have created while getting some useful feedback.

Stick to the plan for your presentation, but be sure to leave time for questions.

With all the tools and technology available to you today, it's possible to create an amazing digital book presentation. This presentation can be shared with your class. It can also be shared on the Web. All in all, it gives you the opportunity to have some fun with your book report while putting your creativity to work. It's a great way to demonstrate what you know while giving your audience good reason to pay attention and give the book a try.

GLOSSARY

APPLICATION A computer program designed to accomplish a purpose; also called an app.

ARTIFACT A man-made object, especially one of historical or cultural interest.

AVATAR A digital image that represents a person online.

CONVENTIONAL Traditional; not original or leading edge.

CUSTOMIZE To make or alter according to individual specifications.

DEVICE A tool or object used for a specific purpose.

EMBED To insert multimedia content such as graphics or audio into a computer program or Web page.

ENTICING Attracting someone to your purpose.

ENVISION To picture or imagine someone or something.

FORMAT A method of organizing information.

FULFILL To meet the requirements of.

FUNDAMENTAL Of or relating to the foundation; basic.

GARNER To gather or acquire.

GENRE A class or category of literature, art, or music.

MULTIMEDIA The combined use of several media, such as text, video, and sound.

PRESENTATION A verbal report accompanied by supporting material to help illustrate points.

STORYBOARD A series of rough sketches that show the way the action will progress in a film, television show, animation, etc.

SYNOPSIS A brief summary of the plot.

VISUALIZING Forming an image in one's mind.

Digital Media and Learning Research Hub
University of California Humanities Research Institute
4000 Humanities Gateway
Irvine, CA 92697-3350
(949) 824-8180
Web site: http://dmlhub.net
This research center studies the impact of digital media on young people's
learning.

International Reading Association
444 North Capitol Street NW, Suite 640
Washington, DC 20001
(202) 624-8800
Web site: http://www.reading.org
This organization promotes reading by advancing the quality of literacy
instruction and research worldwide. Topics of interest include using the
Internet and digital tools to support literacy development.

Photographic Society of America
3000 United Founders Boulevard, Suite 103
Oklahoma City, OK 73112
(405) 843-1437
Web site: http://www.psa-photo.org
The Photographic Society of America is dedicated to educating and connect-
ing people through photography. It has youth programs dedicated to
involving the next generation in photography.

Scholastic Inc.
557 Broadway
New York, NY 10012
(212) 343-6100
Web site: http://www.scholastic.com
Scholastic is the largest publisher and distributor of children's books in the
world. You'll find a number of book talks on its Web site. You can view
these for ideas or to see how others have implemented different
approaches.

Toastmasters International
P.O. Box 9052
Mission Viejo, CA 92690-9052
(949) 858-8255
Web site: http://www.toastmasters.org
Toastmasters International is dedicated to helping people develop their
public speaking and presentation skills. It offers a variety of free
resources to help beginning speakers get started.

YOUmedia Chicago
Harold Washington Library Center
400 S. State Street
Chicago, IL 60605
(312) 747-5260
Web site: http://youmediachicago.org
YOUmedia is an innovative teen learning space in Chicago public libraries.
Teens can access computers, media creation tools, and software that
allow them to stretch their imaginations and digital media skills.

Mentors lead workshops to help teens build skills and create digital projects.

Young Adult Library Services Association (YALSA)
50 East Huron Street
Chicago, IL 60611-2795
(800) 545-2433
Web site: http://www.ala.org/yalsa
A division of the American Library Association (ALA), YALSA is a national association of library professionals working to expand and strengthen library services for teens. As part of its mission, it works to improve digital services for teens in libraries across the country.

WEB SITES

Due to the changing nature of Internet links, Rosen Publishing has developed an online list of Web sites related to the subject of this book. This site is updated regularly. Please use this link to access the list:

http://www.rosenlinks.com/WBPP/Book

Bullard, Lisa. *Ace Your Oral or Multimedia Presentation* (Ace It!). Berkeley Heights, NJ: Enslow Publishers, 2009.

Carlson, Jeff. *The iMovie '11 Project Book: Stuff You Can Do with iMovie.* Berkeley, CA: Peachpit Press, 2011.

Coleman, Miriam. *Present It: Understanding Contexts and Audiences* (Core Skills). New York, NY: PowerKids Press, 2013.

Diamond, S. *Prezi for Dummies.* Hoboken, NJ: Wiley, 2010.

Duarte, Nancy. *Slide:ology: The Art and Science of Creating Great Presentations.* Sebastopol, CA: O'Reilly, 2008.

Durdik, G. *iLife '11 Made Simple.* Berkeley, CA: Apress, 2011.

Furgang, Adam. *Searching Online for Image, Audio, and Video Files* (Digital and Information Literacy). New York, NY: Rosen Central, 2010.

Gallo, Carmine. *Talk Like Ted: The 9 Public Speaking Secrets of the World's Top Minds.* New York, NY: St. Martin's Press, 2014.

Green, Julie. *Shooting Video to Make Learning Fun* (Information Explorer: Super Smart Information Strategies). Ann Arbor, MI: Cherry Lake Publishing, 2011.

Halpern, Monica. *Writing a Book Report.* New York, NY: Scholastic, 2011.

Hutsko, Joe, and Drew Davidson. *Flip Video for Dummies.* Hoboken, NJ: Wiley, 2010.

Murray, Katherine. *My Evernote.* Indianapolis, IN: Que, 2012.

Orr, Tamra. *Creating Multimedia Presentations* (Digital and Information Literacy). New York, NY: Rosen Central, 2010.

Truesdell, Ann. *Make Your Point: Creating Powerful Presentations* (Information Explorer: Super Smart Information Strategies). Ann Arbor, MI: Cherry Lake Publishing, 2013.

BIBLIOGRAPHY

Animoto Inc. "Animoto—Make & Share Beautiful Videos Online." 2013. Retrieved March 7, 2013 (http://animoto.com).

Apple Inc. "Apple—iWork—Keynote—Create Captivating Presentations Easily." 2013. Retrieved March 7, 2013 (http://www.apple.com /iwork/keynote).

Apple Inc. "iLife—iMovie—Read About Movie Trailers and More New Features." 2013. Retrieved March 7, 2013 (http://www.apple.com /ilife/imovie).

CrunchBase. "Juxio." 2013. Retrieved March 17, 2013 (http://www .crunchbase.com/company/juxio).

Doyne, Shannon, and Katherine Schulten. "Beyond the Book Report: Ways to Respond to Literature Using *New York Times* Models." NYTimes. com, November 10, 2011. Retrieved March 14, 2013 (http:// learning.blogs.nytimes.com/2011/11/10/beyond-the-book-report-ways-to-respond-to-literature-using-new-york-times-models).

GoAnimate. "Make a Video. Amazing Animated Video Maker." GoAnimate.com, 2013. Retrieved March 7, 2013 (http://goani-mate.com).

Kemenczy, Kalman. "What Is Prezi?—The Official Intro Video." YouTube. com, April 13, 2010. Retrieved March 12, 2013 (http://www. youtube.com/watch?v=pxhqDOhNx4Q).

LittleBirdTales. "Little Bird Tales—Home." 2013. Retrieved March 7, 2013 (http://littlebirdtales.com).

Macheads101. "iMovie Tutorial." YouTube.com, October 24, 2008. Retrieved March 7, 2013 (http://www.youtube.com/watch?v=5YbA-g1meCg).

Microsoft. "Microsoft PowerPoint—Slide Presentation Software." Office.com, 2013. Retrieved March 7, 2013 (http://office.microsoft.com/en-us /powerpoint).

Nulab Inc. "Cacoo—Create Diagrams Online Real-Time Collaboration—Tour." Cacoo.com, 2013. Retrieved March 12, 2013 (https://cacoo.com/lang/en/tour?ref=header).

Oddcast Inc. "Voki Home." Voki.com, 2013. Retrieved March 7, 2013 (http://www.voki.com).

Officialvoki. "Introducing: Voki Classroom." YouTube.com, August 5, 2011. Retrieved March 7, 2013 (http://www.youtube.com/watch?v=pZwQTm_5s6Q).

Prezi Inc. "Ideas Matter." 2013. Retrieved March 1, 2013 (http://prezi.com).

Smore.com. "Smore—Design Beautiful Online Flyers and Publish Instantly." 2013. Retrieved March 30, 2013 (https://www.smore.com).

SnackTools.com. "SlideSnack—The Secret to Amazing Presentations." YouTube.com, December 15, 2011. Retrieved March 7, 2013 (http://www.youtube.com/watch?v=zHe-WU44PW8).

SnackTools.com. "SlideSnack—Upload & Share Presentations Online." 2013. Retrieved March 7, 2013 (http://www.slidesnack.com).

Storybird.com. "Storybird—Artful Storytelling." Retrieved March 7, 2013 (http://storybird.com).

Stupeflix. "Features—Stupeflix." 2013. Retrieved March 7, 2013 (http://studio.stupeflix.com/en/features).

Sukoneck, Carol. "Google Presentation." YouTube.com, February 27, 2011. Retrieved March 7, 2013 (http://www.youtube.com/watch?v=IDhtMUpX_78).

Tsotsis, Alexia. "Share Combined Images and Text in a Snap with Juxio." TechCrunch.com, August 12, 2010. Retrieved March 7, 2013 (http://techcrunch.com/2010/08/12/share-combined-images-and-text-in-a-snap-with-juxio).

WeVideo Inc. "Overview—WeVideo." 2013. Retrieved March 7, 2013 (http://www.wevideo.com/overview).

INDEX

ABOUT THE AUTHOR

Gina Hagler teaches writing to children in grades K–12 through the KidWrite! program, which she created. She has written several nonfiction books for children and young adults, as well as a number of feature stories for *Odyssey*, *Appleseed*, and *Faces* magazines. As a writer, she has produced podcasts, book trailers, and presentations for her own work. She lives in the Maryland suburbs with her family.

PHOTO CREDITS

Cover © iStockphoto.com/4774344sean; p. 5 Eric Audras/Onoky/Getty Images; p. 7 Roy Mehta/Riser/Getty Images; pp. 8–9 Ron and Patty Thomas /Taxi/Getty Images; p. 12 imago stock&people/Newscom; p. 15 Robert Daly /OJO+/Getty Images; pp. 16–17 © Cleve Bryant/PhotoEdit; p. 19 Geri Lavrov/Photographer's Choice RF/Getty Images; p. 20 GDA/AP Images; p. 24 © Animoto; p. 26 Oddcast, Inc.; p. 30 James Woodson/Photodisc /Thinkstock; p. 33 John Nordell/Christian Science Monitor/Getty Images; p. 35 Photo and Co/The Image Bank/Getty Images; p. 38 © iStockphoto .com/asiseeit; cover and interior graphics (arrows) © iStockphoto.com /artvea.

Designer: Nicole Russo; Editor: Andrea Sclarow Paskoff;
Photo Researcher: Marty Levick